D1065199

FIGURE SKATING

Published in the United States of America by Cherry Lake Publishing
Ann Arbor, Michigan
www.cherrylakepublishing.com

Content Adviser: Liv Williams, Editor, www.iLivExtreme.com
Reading Adviser: Marla Conn MS, Ed., Literacy specialist, Read-Ability, Inc.

Photo Credits: ©Iurii Osadchi / Shutterstock.com, cover, 10, 13, 16, 18, 21, 25; ©Falcon Eyes / Shutterstock.com, 5; ©Jody. / Shutterstock.com, 6; ©Photo from The Fourth Olympiad 1908 London Official Report [1908] / Wikimedia Commons / Public Domain, 7; ©Photographed by Billedbladet NÅ [1955] / Riksarkivet (National Archives of Norway) / flickr.com, 9; ©Rich Moffitt / flickr.com, 15; ©Olga Besnard / Shutterstock.com, 17; ©Paolo Bona / Shutterstock.com, 22; ©Andrey Malgin / Shutterstock.com, 27; ©StockphotoVideo / Shutterstock.com, 28

Library of Congress Cataloging-in-Publication Data

Names: Labrecque, Ellen, author.
Title: Figure skating / Ellen Labrecque.
Description: Ann Arbor, Michigan : Cherry Lake Publishing, 2018. | Series: Global citizens. Olympic sports | Includes bibliographical references and index. | Audience: Grade 4 to 6.
Identifiers: LCCN 2017033727 | ISBN 9781534107564 (hardcover) | ISBN 9781534109544 (pdf) | ISBN 9781534108554 (pbk.) | ISBN 9781534120532 (hosted ebook)
Subjects: LCSH: Figure skating—Juvenile literature. | Olympics—Juvenile literature. | Civics—Juvenile literature.
Classification: LCC GV850.4 .L32 2018 | DDC 796.91/2—dc23
LC record available at https://lccn.loc.gov/2017033727

Cherry Lake Publishing would like to acknowledge the work of The Partnership for 21st Century Learning. Please visit *www.p21.org* for more information.

Printed in the United States of America
Corporate Graphics

ABOUT THE AUTHOR

Ellen Labrecque has written over 100 books for children. She loves the Olympics and has attended both the Winter and Summer Games as a reporter for magazines and television. She lives in Yardley, Pennsylvania, with her husband, Jeff, and her two young "editors," Sam and Juliet. When she isn't writing, she is running, hiking, and reading.

TABLE OF CONTENTS

CHAPTER 1

History: Figure Skating

The first Winter Olympics was held in Chamonix, France, from January 25 to February 5, 1924. It included 258 athletes from 16 different countries competing in 16 events. Since then, the Winter Olympics has been held every 4 years in a number of countries. (The Games were skipped in 1940 and 1944 during World War II.) As the Games progressed, more competitors and events were added. Fast-forward to the 2014 Winter Games held in Sochi, Russia. There were 2,873 competitors from 88 different countries competing in 98 events. That's a lot more competitors and events!

Early ice skate blades were strapped on to shoes.

From jaw-dropping aerial flips in snowboarding to lightning-speed action in hockey, the Winter Games display some of the most unbelievable sports and athletes. Figure skating, one of the most graceful sports in the Winter Olympics, draws some of the biggest crowds in all of the Games.

Skating on ice was once a form of transportation.

The Story of Figure Skating

People ice-skated as far back as 3000 BCE. They used their skates to travel on frozen rivers and lakes. The word *skate* comes from the German word *schake*, which means "leg bone." Ice skates were named this because early skates were made from the leg bones of large animals!

The British discovered that skating didn't have to be only about transportation; it could also be a fun **recreational** activity. They came up with the idea of carving forms, such as circles and

Ulrich Salchow of Denmark won the first gold medal in individual figure skating at the 1908 Games.

figure eights, into the ice while on skates. This is how figure skating got its name. In early competitions, skaters were scored based on the **etchings** they made in the ice with their blades. Figure skating was part of the 1908 Olympic Games, before the Winter Olympics even started. "Figure" skating—or tracing patterns—was what the skaters were judged on.

Developing Claims and Using Evidence

*Scoring in figure skating is based on points. Skaters receive two marks when they skate. One is the technical score. This score looks at how well athletes perform their jumps and spins. The other is the program **components** score. This score looks at the difficulty level of the athlete's performance. Many fans think the scoring is too complicated and hard to understand. Using the Internet and your local library, find out more about figure skating judging at the Olympics. Do you think there is a way to make the scoring fairer and simpler to understand? Why or why not?*

Figure skater Sonja Henie of Norway competed in four Winter Olympics: the 1924, 1928 (gold), 1932 (gold), and 1936 Games (gold).

Before 2004, women were required to wear skirts during figure skating competitions.

The Winter Olympics was first broadcast on television in 1956. Fans found the figure tracing part of the sport boring, but they loved watching the acrobatic leaps and twists. Because of this, figure tracing was eliminated from the event and replaced with a short program and a long program that included skaters jumping and spinning over the ice.

Events

At the 2018 Games in PyeongChang, South Korea, figure skaters will compete in several different events. Most events are scored on their jumps, lifts, and spins. The skater or pair with the highest score wins. Here's a rundown of what they are:

Men's and Women's Singles	Each skater performs a short program and a free skating program. The short program for both men and women is 2 minutes and 50 seconds long. The free skating program is 4 minutes and 30 seconds for men and 4 minutes for women.
Pairs Skating	Just as in the singles program, the pairs perform a short program and a free skating program.
Ice Dancing Mixed	This is like ballroom dancing on ice. This is the only event in which athletes can use music with words. The skating pair is judged more on the quality of the dance than on the acrobatic twists and jumps.
Team Event	Scores from individual skaters are added together.

CHAPTER 2

Geography: Figure Skating Around the World

At the 2014 Winter Olympics held in Sochi, 149 athletes from 30 nations participated in at least one of the figure skating events. For the first time ever, figure skaters from the warm countries of Brazil and the Philippines joined the competition, but they did not win any medals.

Where do the best figure skaters in the world come from? Which countries have won the most Olympic figure skating medals? Which country surprised the world?

Michael Christian Martinez of the Philippines was the first of his country to compete in men's singles at the 2014 Games.

United States

The United States has won a total of 49 Olympic figure skating medals to date, including 15 gold. However, the United States has slipped in recent years, especially in the men's and women's singles event. The country has not won an Olympic medal in women's singles since the 2006 Games (Sasha Cohen, silver). The US team also has not won a medal in men's singles since the 2002 Games (Timothy Goebel, bronze). Experts believe part of the reason the United States isn't performing as well as it once was is because other countries pay their figure skaters to train, while the United States does not.

Cohen started as a gymnast before switching to figure skating.

Tatiana Volosozhar and Maxim Trankov of Russia compete at the 2014 Games.

At 15 years old, Yulia Lipnitskaya was the youngest Russian athlete to take home gold at the 2014 Winter Games.

Russia

Russia has won 26 Olympic figure skating medals, including 14 gold. But Russia was part of the Soviet Union until 1991, when the Soviet Union disbanded. If Russia's total (26) were added to the number of medals the Soviet Union had received until then (24), it would be more than the United States' total. At the 2014 Games, Russia captured the gold in women's singles, the gold and silver in pairs, and the gold in the team event. Russia pays its figure skaters while they train, and it's enough money to support not only themselves, but also their families.

Ten also competed in the 2010 Games.

Kazakhstan

Denis Ten of Kazakhstan won his country's first ever figure skating medal when he captured the bronze at the 2014 Games in the men's singles competition. The best part was that Kazakhstan pays its athletes more money for winning a medal than any other Winter Olympics country. Ten brought home $75,000 for winning the bronze!

Gathering and Evaluating Sources

The Soviet Union was once the largest country in the world, covering over 8.6 million square miles (22.3 million square kilometers). It was two and a half times bigger than the United States! Using the Internet or your local library, find a map of the former Soviet Union. Name the countries today that were once a part of it. Why do you think Russia and the Soviet Union are often associated together? Use the data you find to support your answer.

CHAPTER 3

Civics: Olympic Pride

Hosting the Olympic Games can be a big source of pride for the city and the people who live there. It gives the citizens a chance to show off where they live to the entire world. Also, the athletes and fans who come to the Games spend a lot of money there. One of the biggest ways the host country shows off is at the opening and closing ceremonies. More than 3 billion people watched the opening of the 2014 Winter Games! One of the top ticket demand events in Sochi was figure skating.

The figure skating gala exhibition is a final, non-judged event that allows the athletes to perform one last time.

Shizuka Arakawa of Japan is the first figure skater of her country to win gold at the Olympics.

Figure Skating Popularity

While more Americans ski than figure skate, their favorite sport to watch in all of the Games is figure skating. Nearly three-quarters of all Americans—178 million!—watched figure skating during the 2014 Winter Olympics.

The country that really goes the craziest for figure skating is Japan. Japanese fans even show up at their skaters' warm-ups and practices just to cheer them on. Their passion was rewarded when Yuzuru Hanyu of Japan won the men's singles at the 2014 Games. He arrived home to a parade in his honor, and 100,000 people lined the roads to cheer for him!

The Ambassadors

Olympic cities ask athletes to be **ambassadors** for their Games. The athletes promote the Olympics to fans around the world. One of the ambassadors of the 2018 Games is South Korean figure skater Yuna Kim. Kim is one of her country's most famous athletes. She won gold at the 2010 Olympics in Vancouver, Canada, and silver at the 2014 Games in Sochi. Although she is now retired, she continues to champion figure skating all over the world.

Developing Claims

"Country changing" in figure skating happens a lot. This is when figure skaters become citizens of another country so they have a better chance of competing in the Olympics. The International Skating Union has set up rules that skaters must wait at least two years between representing different countries. Do you think figure skaters should be allowed to switch countries? Or should skaters only be allowed to compete for the country in which they were born? Why or why not?

CHAPTER 4

Economics: Figure Skating Is Big Business

Hosting the Olympic Games costs a lot of money. PyeongChang, the host of the 2018 Winter Olympics, has spent $85 million to build the Gangneung Ice Arena, the **venue** for figure skating. This cost doesn't include any of the other venues or even the stadium for the opening and closing ceremonies. The city hopes to earn back a lot of that money once the Olympics begins.

The Fans

Tourists come to the city to see the Olympics. They spend money by staying in hotels, buying souvenirs, and eating in the city's restaurants. The chance to see figure skating's top stars is

Figure skating fans come to see the different costumes and gravity-defying moves of their favorite athletes.

one of the biggest draws. Tickets for figuring skating events at the Games are always among the most expensive—at the 2018 Games, prices run from $131 to $700 per ticket. That's a lot of money for one ticket!

The Sponsors

Advertisers like Coca-Cola and McDonald's pay a lot of money to sponsor the Olympics. Their signs and logos appear in television commercials and on boards all over the venues. Many clothing companies supply the athletes' uniforms and their outfits for the opening and closing ceremonies. Figure skaters are different, though, when it comes to what they wear during the competition. They all wear their own specially designed costumes. Each costume can cost anywhere from $1,500 to $3,000 per outfit. And many skaters wear more than one at every Olympic event! Some skaters spend as much as $10,000 a year on clothing alone. American figure skater Ashley Wagner's outfit turned heads at the 2014 Olympics. Her original yellow dress was redesigned at the last minute to convey confidence. Her costume designer, Jan Longmire, called it Wagner's "suit of armor."

Taking Informed Action

Do you want to learn more about the Winter Olympics and figure skating? There are many different organizations that you can explore. Check them out online. Here are three to help you start your search:

- *US Figure Skating: Learn more about the national governing body for figure skating in the United States.*
- *Learn to Skate USA—Just for Kids: Find ice rinks and figure skating events near you, and learn more about the rules and skills.*
- *NBC Olympics: Stay updated on all things related to the Winter Olympics.*

Wagner's original yellow dress before being updated for the 2014 Games.

Davis and White of Michigan have been skating together
since they were 9 and 10 years old.

Prize Money

Many athletes around the world receive money from their government to live and train for the Olympics. The United States is one country that doesn't financially support its Olympic athletes when they train. Instead, the country relies on sponsors to give athletes money. The United States does reward athletes once they win a medal. The government pays $25,000 for a gold medal, $15,000 for silver, and $10,000 for bronze. At the 2014 Games, ice dancing pair Meryl Davis and Charlie White each got $25,000 for winning the gold medal, and the US team of eight skaters (including Davis and White) got $10,000 each for winning the bronze medal in the team competition.

Communicating Conclusions

Before reading this book, did you know a lot about figure skating and the Winter Olympics? Now that you know more, would you change anything about the sport? Share what you think with friends at school or with your family at home.

Think About It

There are over 181,000 US Figure Skating members in over 700 clubs across the nation. Women make up approximately 74 percent of the membership and men make up the remaining 25 percent (1 percent is unknown). Eighty-four percent of figure skating fans are women. The remaining 16 percent of fans are men. Why do you think there are significantly more women than men who practice and watch figure skating? Use the data you find from your local library or the Internet to support your answer.

For More Information

Further Reading

MacKay, Jenny. *Figure Skating.* Farmington Hills, MI: Lucent Books, 2012.

Wallechinsky, David, and Jaime Loucky. *The Complete Book of the Winter Olympics.* Hertford, NC: Crossroad Press, 2014.

Waxman, Laura Hamilton. *Figure Skating.* Mankato, MN: Amicus Ink, 2017.

Websites

The International Olympic Committee
https://www.olympic.org/the-ioc
Learn more about how the IOC works to build a better world through sports.

International Skating Union
www.isu.org/en/home
Discover more about figure skating competitions all over the world.

Team USA
www.teamusa.org
Learn all about the US Olympic team.

GLOSSARY

ambassadors (am-BAS-uh-derz) representatives for something, like the Olympics

components (kuhm-POH-nuhnts) parts of a larger whole

etchings (ECH-ingz) carvings or marks made on a surface, such as ice

figure eights (FIG-yur AYTS) dance patterns that resemble the number eight

recreational (rek-ree-AY-shuhn-al) of, relating to, or characteristic of activities like games, sports, or hobbies that you like to do in your spare time

tourists (TOOR-ists) people who are traveling for pleasure

venue (VEN-yoo) the place of an action or event

INDEX